Substituting Ingredients

A Cooking Reference Book

Becky Sue Epstein
Hilary Dole Klein

The Globe Pequot Press

Chester, Connecticut 06412

Library of Congress Cataloging-in-Publication Data

Epstein, Becky Sue, 1952–
    Substituting ingredients.

    Includes index.
    1. Food substitutes. 2. Cookery. I. Klein, Hilary
Dole, 1945–   II. Title.
TX357.E67 1986   641.5   86-45573
ISBN 0-88742-101-6

Manufactured in the United States of America
First Edition/Second Printing, August 1987

CONTENTS

ABOUT
THE AUTHORS

Becky Sue Epstein is a restaurant reviewer for the *Los Angeles Times*. She is also a freelance writer and book critic.

Hilary Dole Klein is a writer for the *Santa Barbara News and Review* and *Santa Barbara Magazine*. She is the editor of *A Guide to Non-Sexist Children's Books*, two editions of *Craft Digest* and *Dr. Sheffrin's Naturopathic Physician's Cookbook*.

INTRODUCTION

DON'T HAVE AN INGREDIENT?   SUBSTITUTE!

DON'T LIKE SOMETHING?   SUBSTITUTE!

CAN'T AFFORD IT?   SUBSTITUTE!

Sunday morning. You wake up strangely filled with energy. You decide to make pancakes as a special treat for the family—the fluffy, yet substantial kind of pancakes your mother made on Sundays. You can almost taste them. You reach for the cookbook where the recipe is marked by a turned-down, much-bespattered page.

"Sour Milk Griddle Cakes," it says. You stop: who, in his or her right mind, keeps sour milk around? You can almost feel the pancake's softness in your mouth, smothered with real Vermont maple syrup. That's the only pancake recipe you want to use. What should you do?

Friday evening. It's a wonderful meal, straight out of Julia Child (well, almost). Fit for a king. Fit, you hope, for an enchanting business dinner that will eventually bring you all the projects, raises and promotions you've dreamed of. It's 7:30. The guests are due any moment. The sauce needs only one final touch to complete its superb flavor. You reach for the cognac to dash in the required two tablespoons. Then you stop. You recall Cousin Don finished off the cognac last weekend, so there isn't any in the house. What now?

Whether on a desert island, in a rented vacation cottage or at home with no time for a trip to the store, everyone has, at sometime, been in this predicament: the recipe you're making calls for an ingredient you don't happen to have on hand.

After we became frantic with problems like this once too often, we decided to do something about it. Something that we, as well as our friends, could benefit by: a book of substitutions. A year of research, questioning and testing later, here it is, for everyone to use.

With this guide in your kitchen, you need not despair. Just look up the next best thing and continue on with your cooking and baking.

Simple? Yes!

You know what you like, what kind of diet your family is on, what the people you're cooking for prefer, so use your own judgment when you choose between substitutes for a given ingredient. Generally, these are substitutions, not exact equivalents.

**REMEMBER: IT'S BETTER TO SUBSTITUTE
THAN TO OMIT**

Substituting Ingredients

MEASUREMENT EQUIVALENTS

For your convenience, here is a list of commonly used measuring equivalents for the kitchen, including:

Baking Pans

Dry and Liquid Measures

Food Measuring Equivalents

Metric Equivalents

Temperatures

BAKING PAN SIZES

NOTE: adjust baking times when changing pan sizes.

Round Cake Pans

8 inches by 1½ inches

= 4 cups

= 50 square inches

= 20 centimeters by 4 centimeters

= 325 square centimeters

9 inches by 1½ inches

= 6 cups

= 64 square inches

= 23 centimeters by 4 centimeters

= 415 square centimeters

Rectangular Cake Pans

8 inches by 8 inches by 2 inches
- = 6 cups
- = 64 square inches
- = 20 centimeters by 20 centimeters by 5 centimeters
- = 415 square centimeters

9 inches by 9 inches by 1½ inches
- = 8 cups
- = 81 square inches
- = 23 centimeters by 23 centimeters by 4 centimeters
- = 525 square centimeters

9 inches by 9 inches by 2 inches
- = 10 cups
- = 81 square inches
- = 23 centimeters by 23 centimeters by 5 centimeters
- = 525 square centimeters

13 inches by 9 inches by 2 inches
- = 14 cups
- = 117 square inches
- = 33 centimeters by 23 centimeters by 5 centimeters
- = 755 square centimeters

Pie Pans

8 inches by 1¼ inches
- = 3 cups, level
- = 4½ cups, mounded
- = 20 centimeters by 3 centimeters

9 inches by 1½ inches
- = 4 cups, level
- = 5 to 6 cups, mounded
- = 23 centimeters by 4 centimeters

Loaf Pans

8½ inches by 4½ inches by 2½ inches
- = 6 cups
- = 22 centimeters by 11 centimeters by 6 centimeters

9 inches by 5 inches by 3 inches
- = 8 cups
- = 23 centimeters by 13 centimeters by 8 centimeters

DRY MEASURES

1 pinch = ⅛ teaspoon (approximately)

½ Tablespoon = 1½ teaspoons

3 teaspoons = 1 Tablespoon

⅙ cup = 2 Tablespoons plus 2 teaspoons

¼ cup = 4 Tablespoons

⅓ cup = 5 Tablespoons plus 1 teaspoon

⅜ cup = 6 Tablespoons

½ cup = 8 Tablespoons

⅔ cup = 10 Tablespoons plus 2 teaspoons

¾ cup = 12 Tablespoons

1 cup = 16 Tablespoons

4 cups = 1 quart

8 quarts = 1 peck*

4 pecks = 1 bushel*

*for large fruits or vegetables, not berries

FOOD MEASURING EQUIVALENTS

NOTE: Measurements may vary, depending on sizes of fruits, vegetables and nuts.

Almonds, 1 lb. shelled = 1 to 1½ cups
1 lb. in shells = 3½ cups

Apples, 1 lb. = 2 large apples
= 2½ to 3 cups sliced

Baking chocolate,
1 square = 1 ounce

Bananas, 1 lb. = 3 to 4 whole
= 2 cups mashed

Beans, 1 lb. dried = 1½ to 2 cups
= 5 to 6 cups cooked

Bread, 1 lb. = 10 to 14 slices
1 slice = ½ cup soft bread crumbs
= ¼ to ⅓ cup dry bread crumbs

Butter, 1 lb. = 4 sticks
= 2 cups

Cabbage, 1 lb. = 4 cups shredded raw
= 2 cups cooked

Carrots, 1 lb. = 3 cups shredded raw

Celery, 1 stalk = ⅓ cup diced

Cheese, 4 ounces = 1 cup shredded

Chocolate chips,
1 12-ounce
package = 2 cups

Coffee, 1 lb. ground = 80 Tablespoons

Cottage cheese, 1 lb. = 2 cups

Cream, heavy (or
whipping, 1 cup) = 2 cups whipped

Dates, 1 lb. = 2⅔ cups chopped, pitted

Eggs, 1 cup = 4 to 5 large
= 8 to 10 whites
= 10 to 12 yolks

Figs, 1 lb. = 2⅔ cups chopped

Flour, 1 lb. white = 3½ to 4 cups

1 cup white = 1 cup plus 2 Tablespoons cake flour

1 lb. cake = 4 to 4½ cups

1 cup cake = ⅞ cup white flour

1 lb. whole wheat = 3 cups sifted

Green pepper, 1 large = 1 cup diced

Honey, 1 lb. = 1⅓ cups

Lemon, 1 medium = 2 to 3 Tablespoons juice

= 1 to 2 teaspoons rind, grated

Macaroni, 1 lb. elbow = 8 to 9 cups cooked

Margarine, 1 lb. = 4 sticks

= 2 cups

Marshmallows, 1 large = 7 miniature

11 large = 1 cup

Mushrooms, 1 lb. fresh = 5 cups sliced

= 12 ounces canned, drained

Noodles, 1 lb. = 6 to 8 cups cooked

MEASUREMENT EQUIVALENTS

Onion, 1 medium = 1¼ cup chopped

Orange, 1 medium = ⅓ to ½ cup juice

= 1 to 2 Table-spoons peel, grated

Peaches, 1 lb. = 4 medium

= 2 cups, sliced, peeled

Peanuts, 1 lb. shelled = 2¼ cups

Peas, 1 lb. in pod = 1 cup shelled

Pecans, 1 lb. shelled = 3 to 4 cups

Potatoes, 1 lb. = 3 medium

= 2¼ cups cooked

= 1¾ cups mashed

Prunes, 1 lb. = 2¼ cups pitted

Raisins, 1 lb. = 2¾ cups

Rice, 1 cup uncooked = 3 cups cooked

1 lb. = 2 to 2½ cups uncooked

Spaghetti, 1 lb.   = 6½ cups cooked

Sugar
  granulated white,
    1 lb.   = 2 cups

  powdered or confectioners,
    1 lb.   = 3½ to 4 cups

  brown, 1 lb.
    firmly packed   = 2¼ cups

Tea, 1 lb. leaves   = 100 servings

Tomatoes, 1 lb.   = 2 to 3 medium

                = 1 8-ounce can

                = 1 cup chopped

Walnuts, English
  1 lb. shelled   = 4 cups
  1 lb. in shell   = 1⅔ cups

LIQUID MEASURES

1 dash = a few drops (approximately)

3 teaspoons = 1 Tablespoon

1 Tablespoon = ½ fluid ounce

2 Tablespoons = 1 fluid ounce

1 jigger = 3 Tablespoons
= 1½ fluid ounces

½ cup = 4 fluid ounces

16 Tablespoons = 1 cup
= 8 fluid ounces

2 cups = 1 pint

2 pints = 1 quart

4 quarts = 1 gallon

Fluid Ounces	=	Milliliters
1		30
2		60
4		120
6		180
8 (1 cup)		235
16 (1 pint)		475
32 (1 quart)		945

NOTE: 1 quart = approximately 1 liter

1 quart = .946 liter

1 liter = 1.057 quarts

METRIC EQUIVALENTS

Ounces	=	Grams
1		28
2		57
3		85
4		113
5		142
6		170
7		198
8		227
9		255
10		284
11		312
12		340
13		368
14		397
15		425
16		454

Grams	=	Ounces
1		.035
50		1.75
100		3.5
250		8.75
500		17.5
750		26.25
1000		35
(1 kilogram)		(2.21 lbs)

MEASUREMENT EQUIVALENTS

Pounds	=	Kilograms
1		.45
2		.91
3		1.4
4		1.8
5		2.3
6		2.7
7		3.2
8		3.5
9		4.1
10		4.5

Kilograms	=	Pounds
1		2.2
2		4.4
3		6.6
4		8.8
5		11

TEMPERATURES

	Degrees Fahrenheit =	Degrees Celsius or Centigrade
Room temperature	70	21
Lukewarm	90	32
Water's Boiling Point	212	100
Low Oven or Cool Oven	250	120
Slow Oven	300	150
Moderately Slow	325	165
Moderate Oven	350	180
Moderately Hot	375	190
Hot Oven	400	205
Very Hot Oven	450–500	230–260
Broil	550	290

BAKING INGREDIENTS

There are a few general things to note about baking.

It's important to remember that substitutions which work in the oven may not work on top of the stove. And vice versa.

Certain substitutions are standard in baking recipes, one of the most obvious being that margarine can be used in place of butter which can be used in place of shortening without noticeably affecting the texture of the baked goods.

Baking times may vary, depending on the substitution, so be sure to monitor items and test for doneness.

Everyone has heard about using whole wheat instead of white flour, or carob rather than chocolate, and all the rest of the "healthful" substitutions, but nutritional improvement is not our purpose here. We do believe in freedom of choice, whether you're out of an ingredient or you want to change a recipe for dietetic reasons. So, where several substitutes are given—though we've tried to list them beginning with the best-tasting (and best-functioning) equivalent—use your own preference as a guide.

BAKING POWDER
(1 teaspoon double-acting)

= ½ teaspoon cream of tartar plus ¼ teaspoon baking soda

= ¼ teaspoon baking soda plus ½ cup sour milk or cream or buttermilk, and delete some other liquid from recipe

= ¼ teaspoon baking soda plus 2 more eggs if recipe calls for sweet milk, and delete some other liquid.

= 1 teaspoon baking soda

= 4 teaspoons quick-cooking tapioca

BAKING POWDER
(1 teaspoon single-acting)

= ¾ teaspoon double acting baking powder

BROWN SUGAR (½ cup)

= ½ cup white sugar plus 2 Tablespoons molasses

NOTE: to replace a combination of brown sugar and milk use honey and powdered milk OR molasses and powdered milk.

BUTTER

= margarine

= shortening (salt optional)

See OIL

See DAIRY PRODUCTS CHAPTER

BAKING CHOCOLATE (1 ounce or 1 square), unsweetened

= 3 Tablespoons cocoa powder plus 1 Tablespoon butter or margarine

= 3 Tablespoons carob powder plus 2 Tablespoons water

PRE-MELTED BAKING CHOCOLATE (1 ounce)

= 3 Tablespoons unsweetened cocoa plus 1 Tablespoon oil or melted shortening

SEMI-SWEET CHOCOLATE (6 ounces chips, bits or squares)

= 9 Tablespoons cocoa plus 7 Tablespoons sugar plus 3 Tablespoons shortening

COFFEE (½ cup strong brewed)

= 1 teaspoon instant in ½ cup water

CORN SYRUP (1 cup light)

= 1¼ cups sugar plus ⅓ cup liquid, boiled together till syrupy

EGGS

See DAIRY PRODUCTS CHAPTER

FLOUR (1 cup, WHITE)

= 1 cup plus 2 Tablespoons cake flour

= ¾ cup whole wheat flour, and reduce shortening to ⅔ the amount for cookies; add 1 or 2 more Tablespoons liquid for cakes, add more for bread.
NOTE: This will make the product denser (heavier); it's advisable to start out substituting half whole wheat or other grain flours. Rye, for instance, has a nutty flavor. Soy can also be used for extra protein: substitute 1/10 to 1/4 soy flour for wheat flour

FLOUR, up to a few Tablespoonfuls for thickening

See GENERAL COOKING CHAPTER

GRAHAM FLOUR

= whole wheat flour

HONEY (1 cup)

= 1¼ cups sugar plus ¼ cup more
liquid

NOTE: This may cause the product
to brown faster, and may necessi-
tate a lower oven temperature.

MARGARINE

See BUTTER

See OIL

See SHORTENING

MOLASSES (1 cup)

= ¾ cup sugar (brown or white)
plus ¼ cup liquid

NOTE: increase spices to taste

OIL (1 Tablespoon)

= 1¼ Tablespoons butter

= 1¼ Tablespoons margarine

NOTES:
Use these only for small amounts, up
to a few Tablespoons.

If substituting olive or other strong oils
in baking, add a few drops of mint
to mask their pungency; the baked
goods will have mint flavor, however.

PIE SPICE (PUMPKIN OR APPLE):

½ teaspoon cinnamon

¼ teaspoon nutmeg

⅛ teaspoon allspice

⅛ teaspoon cardamon

¼ teaspoon ground cloves

See HERBS, SPICES AND FLAVORINGS CHAPTER

SELF-RISING FLOUR (1 cup)

= 1 cup flour plus ¼ teaspoon baking powder (optional: pinch of salt)

SEMOLINA FLOUR

= cream of wheat

= farina OR other similar breakfast cereal

SHORTENING, VEGETABLE (1 cup)

= 1 cup butter

= 1 cup margarine .

SUGAR (1 cup GRANULATED WHITE)

= 1 cup turbinado sugar

= 1 cup firmly-packed brown sugar

= 2 cups powdered sugar, sifted

= ¾ cup honey OR 1¼ cups molasses and reduce other liquid in recipe by ¼ cup, or add ¼ cup flour if no other liquid is called for

= 1 cup corn syrup, but never replace more than half the amount of sugar this way, and always reduce the other liquid in the recipe by ¼ cup for each 2 cups sugar substituted this way.

NOTES:

Sugar may generally be reduced by ¼, OR by up to ½ cup if liquid is reduced by ¼ cup.

A few Tablespoons of granulated sugar may be replaced by maple sugar.

Sugar substitutions tend to make baked goods heavier.

Write to manufacturers of artificial sweeteners for recipes using those products.

WHOLE WHEAT FLOUR (1 cup)

= 1 cup graham flour

= 2 Tablespoons wheat germ plus enough white flour to make 1 cup (product may be less dense or lighter with white flour)

See FLOUR

VANILLA EXTRACT

= almond extract

= peppermint extract OR other extracts, which will, of course, alter the flavor of the product.

See HERBS, SPICES AND FLAVORINGS CHAPTER

YEAST (1 envelope dry)

= 1 Tablespoon powdered yeast

= ½ cake compressed yeast, crumbled

CONDIMENTS

When you feel the inclination to spice up your life—or at least your food—it's not hard to mix up any of the condiments below, especially when there's no time to go out and buy an expensively-packaged combination of ingredients.

BAR-B-Q SAUCE

½ cup vinegar

1 cup ketchup

½ cup chopped onion

½ teaspoon cayenne pepper

½ cup brown sugar

2 teaspoons dry mustard

2 Tablespoons Worcestershire sauce

½ cup butter OR vegetable oil

Optional: ½ teaspoon salt

2 Tablespoons liquid smoke

NOTE: simmer ingredients 30 minutes, if desired.

CHUTNEY

1 8-ounce jar preserves—apricot OR peach

1 clove garlic, minced OR ½ teaspoon garlic powder

½ teaspoon powdered ginger

½ teaspoon salt

1 Tablespoon apple cider vinegar

Optional: ¼ cup raisins

COCKTAIL SAUCE

2 Tablespoons horseradish

⅓ cup ketchup

(continued)

Optional: 1½ teaspoons Worcestershire sauce

2 Tablespoons lemon juice

black pepper

bottled hot sauce to taste

½ cup chili sauce

GARLIC BUTTER (½ cup)

1 clove garlic, mashed

4 Tablespoons salted butter, creamed or melted

HERB BUTTER (½ cup)

½ teaspoon parsley

½ teaspoon chives

½ teaspoon tarragon

½ teaspoon shallots

4 Tablespoons salted butter, creamed

HONEY BUTTER (¼ cup)

1 Tablespoon honey

3 Tablespoons unsalted butter, creamed

HONEY MUSTARD (¼ cup)

2 Tablespoons honey

3 Tablespoons prepared yellow mustard

HOT FUDGE SAUCE

Regular Fudge Sauce:

1 egg, slightly beaten

1 cup sugar

¼ cup cream

2 squares unsweetened baking chocolate

Melt all together slowly over low heat.
Bring to boil. Cool a minute.
Beat in 1 Tablespoon butter and
1 teaspoon vanilla.
Serve warm on ice cream.

Bittersweet Fudge Sauce:

4 squares unsweetened baking chocolate

3 Tablespoons butter

⅔ cup water

1¾ cups sugar

¾ cup corn syrup

Melt butter and chocolate slowly over low heat. Add rest of ingredients and boil 10 minutes. Allow to cool a few minutes.

Beat in 1 teaspoon vanilla or rum.
Serve warm.

KETCHUP (½ cup)

½ cup tomato sauce

2 Tablespoons sugar

1 Tablespoon vinegar   (continued)

⅛ teaspoon ground cloves
OR:
½ cup tomato sauce
¼ cup sugar
1 Tablespoon vinegar

MUSTARD (1 Tablespoon prepared)

1 teaspoon dry mustard
½ teaspoon water
2 drops vinegar

SOY SAUCE (¼ cup)

3 Tablespoons Worcestershire sauce
1 Tablespoon water
NOTE: light and dark soy sauce can be substituted for each other.

TARTAR SAUCE (½ cup)

2 Tablespoons chopped pickle relish
OR chopped pickles
6 Tablespoons mayonnaise
Optional: 1 Tablespoon chopped onion
1 Tablespoon chopped hard-boiled egg
a few drops lemon juice

WORCESTERSHIRE SAUCE (1 teaspoon)

1 teaspoon soy sauce
2 drops hot pepper sauce
1 dash lemon juice
1 pinch sugar OR 1 dash molasses

DAIRY PRODUCTS

People have their own preferences; we are brought up with the taste of buttermilk, for instance, instead of cream or yogurt or sour milk in our family's cooking.

Except for whipping, heavy cream and light cream can be used interchangeably. Yogurt or sour cream can be used for a tangier taste or a different fat content, though it's generally not a good idea to boil yogurt or sour cream, as they can separate.

BUTTER (1 cup)

- = 1 cup margarine
- = ⅞ cup vegetable shortening
- = ⅞ cup lard
- = ⅞ cup cottonseed oil
- = ⅞ cup nut oil
- = ⅞ cup corn oil
- = ⅔ cup chicken fat (not for baking or sweets)
- = ⅞ cup solid shortening

NOTES:

For 1 Tablespoon butter use ¾ Tablespoon oil OR 1 Tablespoon bacon grease for frying (this will flavor food, too).

Oil is not generally interchangeable with butter in baking.

For softened butter (or to stretch butter) blend ½ cup corn oil or safflower oil into 1 lb. butter; refrigerate.

BUTTERMILK

- = 1 cup milk plus 1¾ Tablespoons cream of tartar
- = sour cream

CLOTTED CREAM

= heavy cream

= sour cream with pinch of baking soda

= creme fraiche

COTTAGE CHEESE

= ricotta cheese

= yogurt, especially in dips

= cream cheese

CREAM CHEESE

= cottage cheese blended with cream OR cream with a little butter and/or milk to correct consistency

CREME FRAICHE

= sour cream, in recipes

= sour cream, with pinch of baking soda added, to "sweeten"

NOTE: To make creme fraiche:

2 cups heavy cream

add 1 cup buttermilk OR sour milk OR yogurt

stir well; heat to 80 degrees, no higher; pour into container; cover and let sit at least 6–8 hours; then refrigerate.

EGG (1 whole)

- = 2 Tablespoons liquid plus 2 Table- spoons flour plus ½ Tablespoon shortening plus ½ teaspoon bak- ing powder
- = 2 yolks plus 1 Tablespoon water
- = just 2 egg yolks, in custards or similar mixtures
- = 2 Tablespoons oil plus 1 Tablespoon water
- = 1 teaspoon cornstarch and use 3 Tablespoons more liquid in recipe

NOTES:

If halving recipe, do not try to halve eggs; if you must halve eggs, use white only for half an egg.

If short 1 egg in recipe, substitute 1 teaspoon vinegar or 1 teaspoon baking powder.

EGG WHITES (2)

- = 1 egg and ½ Tablespoon shorten- ing, minus 1 Tablespoon liquid

NOTE: this is not for egg whites to be whipped.

EVAPORATED MILK

> = light cream (half-and-half)
>
> = heavy cream

FARMER CHEESE (also known as WHITE CHEESE)

> = cottage cheese
>
> = ricotta cheese
>
> = cream cheese

HALF AND HALF

> See LIGHT CREAM

HEAVY CREAM (1 cup, not for whipping)

> = ¾ cup milk plus ⅓ cup butter or margarine
>
> = ¾ cup milk plus ¼ cup shortening or butter
>
> = ⅔ cup evaporated milk

LIGHT CREAM (1 cup; also called HALF AND HALF)

> = ½ cup heavy cream plus ½ cup milk
>
> = ⅞ cup milk plus 3 Tablespoons butter or margarine
>
> = ½ cup evaporated milk plus ½ cup milk

MARGARINE

= butter

= shortening

See NOTES under BUTTER

MAYONNAISE

= yogurt OR sour cream, especially in small amounts and in dips

MILK (1 cup)

= 1¼ cup light cream (optional: delete up to 4 Tablespoons shortening from recipe)

= ½ cup evaporated milk plus ½ cup water

= 1 cup skimmed milk (optional: plus 2 Tablespoons shortening)

= 3 Tablespoons powdered milk plus 1 cup water (and add 2 Tablespoons butter, if whole milk required)

= soy or nut milks, in recipes

NOTE: you can use up to 1 cup fruit juice instead of milk, in baking.

RICOTTA CHEESE
- = cottage cheese
- = farmer cheese (white, soft cheese)
- = cream cheese, in small amounts

SHORTENING

See BUTTER or MARGARINE

SOUR CREAM (1 cup)
- = 1 Tablespoon white vinegar plus enough milk to make 1 cup; let stand 5 minutes before using.
- = 1 Tablespoon lemon juice plus enough evaporated milk to make 1 cup
- = 1 cup plain yogurt (especially in dips and cold soups)
- = cottage cheese, mixed with yogurt, if desired, and 2 Tablespoons milk and 1 Tablespoon lemon juice; blend well.
- = ⅓ cup melted butter plus ¾ cup sour milk for baking.
- = 6 ounces cream cheese plus 3 Tablespoons milk

SOUR MILK (1 cup)

= 1½ Tablespoons lemon juice or vinegar plus enough milk to make 1 cup.

WHIPPED CREAM (1 cup, sweetened)

= 1 4-ounce package frozen whipped cream topping

= 1 envelope whipped topping mix, prepared as directed

= 1 mashed banana beaten with 1 stiffly beaten egg white plus 1 teaspoon sugar

= 1 cup nonfat dry milk powder whipped with 1 cup ice water and sweetened to taste. This is for low calorie desserts and drinks; it will not hold firm.

YOGURT (plain)

= sour cream

= creme fraiche

= buttermilk

= heavy cream

= mayonnaise (in small amounts, especially in salads or dips)

FRUITS AND NUTS

When you're looking for grape-flavored bubblegum, nothing else will do, but when you're making a pie, one berry can be as flavorful as the next. And limes are as good as lemons in any recipe we can think of. Both are indispensable—use a splash of their juice, for instance, to keep cut fruits and vegetables from turning brown.

About nuts: some people love them and some can't abide them—you know where you and your family stand on this issue.

APPLES (1 cup, chopped)

= 1 cup chopped, firm pears plus 1 Tablespoon lemon juice

BLACKBERRIES

= boysenberries

= raspberries

BOYSENBERRIES

= blackberies

= raspberries

GRATED COCONUT

NOTE: if less than ½ cup, can be omitted from recipe

CURRANTS (1 cup)

= 1 cup raisins

= 1 cup finely-chopped soft prunes or dates

NOTE: if less than ½ cup, can be omitted from recipe

DATES

> = raisins
>
> = figs
>
> = prunes
>
> **NOTE:** if less than ½ cup, can be omitted from recipe

FIGS

> **NOTE:** if less than ½ cup, can be omitted from recipe

HUCKLEBERRIES

> = blueberries

LEMONS

> = limes

GRATED LEMON PEEL

> = equal amount of marmalade
>
> = equal amount of lime or orange peel
>
> **NOTE:** if less than 1 Tablespoon, can be omitted from recipe

LIMES

> = lemons

MELON

> = papaya
>
> = mango
>
> **CRENSHAW** = SPANISH MELON
>
> **HONEYDEW** = CASABA MELON

NECTARINES

> = peaches

NUTS (in cakes or biscuits)

> = bran
>
> = soy nuts, toasted and chopped, in baking
>
> **NOTE:** if less than ½ cup, can be omitted from recipe

GRATED ORANGE PEEL

> = equal amount of marmalade
>
> = equal amount of lemon peel or lime peel
>
> **NOTE:** if less than 1 Tablespoon can be omitted from recipe

PEACHES

> = nectarines
>
> = cantaloupe (in an ice, primarily)

PEANUT BUTTER
> = sesame paste
> = other nut butters

PEARS
> = apples

PECANS
> = walnuts, in small amounts

PINE NUTS (also called PIGNOLES)
> = chopped walnuts, for pesto and other Mediterranean-type recipes

PIGNOLES
> See PINE NUTS

RAISINS (1 cup)
> = 1 cup currants
> = 1 cup finely-chopped soft prunes or dates

> **NOTE:** if less than ½ cup, can be omitted from recipe

RASPBERRIES
> = blackberries
> = boysenberries

GENERAL COOKING

This chapter is a collection of stove-top substitutions for those moments when your mind goes as blank as your cupboard while you're staring at a recipe.

Certain ingredients are standard substitutions in cooking—though they're not always the same for baking.

Please note, for artificial sweeteners, you must always follow the instructions on the package because the different chemicals can cause different reactions.

ARROWROOT

Up to a few Tablespoons, for
thickening

See FLOUR

ANGEL HAIR PASTA

= vermicelli

= Oriental (ramen) noodles

BEEF BROTH (1 cup)

= 1 bouillon cube plus 1 cup water

= 1 cup beef stock

= 1 cup beef consomme

CHICKEN BROTH (1 cup)

= 1 bouillon cube plus 1 cup water

= 1 cup chicken stock

BLUE CHEESE

= Roquefort cheese

BREAD CRUMBS (¼ cup DRY)

= ¼ cup cracker crumbs

= ½ slice bread, cubed, toasted and crumbled

= ¼ cup rolled oats

= ¼ cup soft bread crumbs

= ¼ cup matzah meal

= ¼ cup flour

BULGAR

= cracked wheat

BUTTER

See DAIRY PRODUCTS CHAPTER

CLUB SODA

= mineral water

= seltzer

COCONUT MILK (1 cup fresh, thick)

= 4 to 5 Tablespoons coconut cream, solidified, dissolved in 1 cup hot water or milk

= 1 cup (top layer of) canned cream of coconut liquid

= 1 cup medium cream with 1 teaspoon coconut flavoring

COCONUT MILK (1 cup fresh, thin)

= 2 Tablespoons coconut cream, solidified, dissolved in 1 cup hot water or milk

= 1 cup canned cream of coconut liquid

= 1 cup whole milk with 1 teaspoon coconut flavoring

= 1 cup milk beaten with 3 Tablespoons grated coconut

CORN FLOUR

Up to a few Tablespoons, for thickening

See FLOUR

CORNSTARCH

Up to a few Tablespoons, for thickening

See FLOUR

EMMENTHALER CHEESE

= Jarlsberg cheese

= Swiss cheese

FLOUR

Up to a few Tablespoons only, primarily for thickening

= Bisquick

= tapioca (quick-cooking, especially)

= cornstarch or corn flour

= arrowroot

= brown rice flour OR soy flour OR rye flour

= potato starch OR potato flour

= mashed potatoes, flakes OR prepared

= 1 whole egg OR 2 yolks OR 2 whites (especially for cooked sauces)

JARLSBERG CHEESE

= Emmenthaler cheese

= Swiss cheese

LEMON JUICE

= vinegar

= lime juice

= crushed vitamin C pills mixed with water to taste (for small amounts).

LIQUEUR

See HERBS, SPICES AND FLAVORINGS CHAPTER

NOTE: 1 liqueur can be used in place of 2 in a recipe

LIME JUICE

= lemon juice

MILK

See DAIRY PRODUCTS CHAPTER

MINERAL WATER

= club soda

= seltzer

OIL

= butter or margarine, to sauté or fry, mostly

Also see BAKING INGREDIENTS CHAPTER

NOTE: burning temperatures of different oils, butter and margarine vary

OLIVE OIL
> = vegetable oils
>
> = sesame oil
>
> = walnut oil
>
> **NOTE:** use half olive, half vegetable oil to reduce pungency of flavor

PARMESAN CHEESE
> = romano cheese

POTATO FLOUR
> Up to a few Tablespoons, for thickening
>
> **See FLOUR**

ROQUEFORT CHEESE
> = blue cheese

ROMANO CHEESE
> = parmesan cheese

SELTZER
> = club soda
>
> = mineral water

SESAME OIL
> = olive oil
>
> = peanut oil

SPAGHETTI
> = spaghettini
>
> = vermicelli
>
> = narrow egg noodles
>
> = other long noodles, including Japanese (ramen) noodles

STOCK (CHICKEN, BEEF, VEAL, FISH)
> = bouillon
>
> = consomme
>
> **NOTE:** stock in a sauce may be replaced by wine for up to one-third of amount of stock called for.

SUGAR (1 cup granulated)
> = 1¾ cups powdered OR confectioners
>
> **See BAKING INGREDIENTS CHAPTER**
>
> **NOTE:** in coffee, flavorings like vanilla and cinnamon can be used instead of sugar.

SWISS CHEESE
> = Jarlsberg cheese
>
> = Emmenthaler cheese

TOMATO JUICE (1 cup)
> = 2 or 3 fresh, ripe tomatoes,

(continued)

peeled, seeded, and blended in blender or food processor; add salt and lemon juice to taste.
= ½ cup tomato sauce plus ½ cup water

TOMATO PASTE (1 Tablespoon)
= 1 Tablespoon ketchup
= ¼ cup tomato sauce (and eliminate some other liquid from recipe)

TOMATO PUREE (1 cup)
= 1 cup tomato sauce
= ⅓ cup tomato paste plus ½ cup water

TOMATO SAUCE (2 cups)
= ¾ cup tomato paste plus 1 cup water
= 2 cups tomato puree

VERMICELLI
= angel hair pasta
= spaghettini
= Japanese (ramen) noodles
= spaghetti OR other long noodles

VINEGAR
= lemon juice, in cooking

HERBS, SPICES AND FLAVORINGS

These are the best equivalents, the closest possible substitutions and, as such, all substitutions are not necessarily judged reciprocally equivalent.

In general, 1 Tablespoon of fresh herbs equals 1 teaspoon of dried herbs. When using dried herbs, crush them in the palm of your hand before adding to the dish; crushing releases their flavors.

NOTE: if using dried substitutions, cook dish 15 minutes after adding, then taste.

A NOTE ABOUT WINES AND SPIRITS: These are used to add flavor; the alcohol evaporates quickly during cooking.

For both red and white wines, stick to the drier, rather than sweet varieties. Madeira, sherry and port are used to add sweetness to specific cooking and baking recipes. Also, be sure to use good brandy or cognac, when either is called for. See listing below for **LIQUEURS.**

ALLSPICE

= black pepper (in cooking)

= ¼ teaspoon cinnamon plus ½
teaspoon cloves, plus ¼ teaspoon nutmeg (It's possible to use
one, two or three of them
together, in baking.)

ANGOSTURA BITTERS

(a secret formula) includes cinnamon, cloves, mace, nutmeg, orange
and/or lemon peel, prunes and rum.

ANISE

= fennel

= dill

= cumin

ANISE SEED (STAR ANISE)

= fennel seed

= caraway seed (use more)

AROMATICS

See FLAVORINGS

See LIQUEURS

AZAFRAN (or SAFFLOWER)

= saffron (use only a tiny bit)

BASIL (dried only)

> = tarragon
>
> = summer savory

BAY LEAF

> = thyme

BOUQUET GARNI

> = 3 stalks parsley, 1 stalk thyme, 1 bay leaf
>
> optional: basil, celery leaf, fennel, marjoram, tarragon and other similar aromatic herbs

BOURBON

> = whiskey

BRANDY

> = cognac
>
> = rum

CAPERS

> = pickled, green nasturtium seeds

CARAWAY SEED

> = fennel seed
>
> = cumin seed

CARDAMOM

= cinnamon

= mace

CELERY SEED

= dill seed

CHERVIL

= parsley

= tarragon (use less)

CHILI POWDER

= cayenne pepper (hot red pepper)

optional: add cumin, oregano, garlic and other spices

CHINESE PARSLEY

See CILANTRO

CHIVES

= green onion (tops)

= onion powder (use small amount)

See VEGETABLES CHAPTER

CILANTRO (or CORIANDER LEAF)

= celery leaf

= parsley (use more)

CINNAMON
> = allspice (use less)
> = cardamom

CLOVES (ground)
> = allspice
> = nutmeg
> = mace

COGNAC
> = brandy

CORIANDER LEAF
> See CILANTRO

CORIANDER (GROUND CORIANDER SEED)
> = caraway plus cumin
> = lemon plus sage

CUMIN
> = ⅓ anise plus ⅔ caraway
> = fennel

CURRY POWDER

2 Tablespoons ground coriander

2 Tablespoons black pepper

2 Tablespoons cumin

2 Tablespoons red pepper

2 Tablespoons turmeric

1¼ teaspoons ground ginger

Optional: allspice, cinnamon, ground fennel, garlic powder, mace

DILL SEED

= celery seed

EXTRACTS

See FLAVORINGS

See LIQUEURS

FENNEL SEED

= anise seed (or star anise)

= caraway seed

FILÉ POWDER

See (GUMBO) FILÉ

FINES HERBES

= equal amounts of parsley,
tarragon,
chervil,
chives

FIVE SPICE POWDER (for Oriental cooking)

= equal amounts of anise,
  fennel,
  cinnamon,
  black pepper,
  cloves

FLAVORINGS (EXTRACTS AND AROMATICS)

commonly available;
some are imitation:

ALMOND

ANISE

BANANA

BRANDY

BUTTER

CHERRY

CHOCOLATE

COCONUT

LEMON

MAPLE

ORANGE

PEPPERMINT

PINEAPPLE

ROSE WATER

ROOT BEER

RUM

VANILLA

See LIQUEURS

GARAM MASALA (for Indian cooking)
2 teaspoons ground cardamom
5 teaspoons ground coriander
4 teaspoons ground cumin
1 teaspoon ground cloves
2 teaspoons black pepper
1 teaspoon ground cinnamon
1 teaspoon ground nutmeg

GARLIC (1 clove)
= ⅛ teaspoon instant minced garlic
= ⅛ teaspoon garlic powder
= ¼ teaspoon garlic juice
= ½ teaspoon garlic salt (and leave ½ teaspoon salt out of dish)
= garlic chives (use more)
See VEGETABLES CHAPTER

GINGER (fresh, grated)
= powdered ginger (use less)
= minced, crystallized ginger with sugar washed off

GINGER (powdered)
= ⅓ mace plus ⅔ lemon peel

(GUMBO) FILÉ
= sassafras

LEMON

= lime

= lemongrass

= verbena

LEMON JUICE

= vinegar

= lime juice

= crushed Vitamin C pills mixed with water to taste (for small amounts).

LEMONGRASS

= lemon

= verbena

LIME

= lemon

LIQUEURS

Standard liqueur flavors include:

Mint—Creme de Menthe

Orange—Curacao, Grand Marnier, Cointreau

Raspberry—Cassis, Chambord

Anise (or licorice)—Pastis, Ouzo, Pernod, Arak

NOTE: 1 liqueur can be used in place of 2 in a recipe

MACE

= allspice

= cloves

= nutmeg (OR nutmeg plus cardamom)

MADEIRA

= sherry

= port

MARJORAM

= oregano (use less)

= thyme

MARINADE FOR BEEF OR LAMB

1 cup red wine (or wine vinegar)

1 cup salad oil or olive oil or combination

2 cloves garlic

1 teaspoon black pepper, freshly ground

¼ cup minced fresh parsley

½ teaspoon dried thyme

½ teaspoon dried marjoram

1 bay leaf

(continued)

Optional:
    1 small onion, chopped
    1 small carrot, chopped
    2 allspice berries, whole
    1 teaspoon salt
    ½ teaspoon dried rosemary

MARINADE FOR CHICKEN

As in preceding recipe, but use dry white wine instead of red

MARINADE FOR FISH OR CHICKEN

1½ cups soy sauce
1¾ cups ketchup
¼ cup dry red wine
2 Tablespoons fresh grated ginger
2 Tablespoons brown sugar
1 small onion, finely chopped
juice of 1 lemon (2 to 3 Tablespoons)
dash of bottled hot sauce
2 cloves garlic, mashed

MARINADE FOR PORK

    1½ cups dry white wine

    3 Tablespoons olive oil

    1 small onion, chopped

    1 bay leaf

    2 whole cloves

    ½ teaspoon dried thyme

    optional:

        1 small carrot, chopped

        2 allspice berries, whole

        2 juniper berries, whole

MINT

    = mint or spearmint tea from tea
       bags or bulk tea

    = creme de menthe, in sweets

MUSTARD (1 teaspoon dry)

    = 1 Tablespoon prepared mustard
       from jar

NUTMEG

    = allspice

    = cloves

    = mace

ONION (1 medium or ¼ cup)

= 1 Tablespoon instant minced onion

= ¼ cup frozen chopped onion

= 1 Tablespoon onion powder

= shallots (use a little more)

= leeks

= green onions (use more)

See VEGETABLES CHAPTER

ONION POWDER

(See preceding)

ORANGE PEEL

= tangerine peel

= marmalade

= Grand Marnier

= Curacao

= Cointreau

= lemon or lime peel

OREGANO

= marjoram

= rosemary

= thyme (fresh)

PAPRIKA

> = turmeric with red (or cayenne) pepper

PARSLEY

> = chervil
> = tarragon

BLACK PEPPER

> = allspice (in cooking, especially if salt is used in dish)

BLACK PEPPERCORNS

> = white peppercorns
> **NOTE:** peppercorns vary in strength

CAYENNE PEPPER

> = ground, hot red pepper
> = chili powder

WHITE PEPPERCORNS

> = black peppercorns
> **NOTE:** peppercorns vary in strength

RED PEPPER (ground)

= cayenne pepper

= chili powder

= hot pepper sauce

= bottled hot sauce

= hot red pepper flakes

HOT RED PEPPER FLAKES

= chopped, dried red pepper pods

= red pepper (use less)

RED PEPPER OIL (for Oriental cooking)

= heat 3 Tablespoons sesame oil; fry 3 to 4 spicy red peppers in it until they turn dark; remove peppers and discard; use oil.

HOT PEPPER SAUCE

= bottled hot sauce

= Tabasco sauce

= ground red pepper

= cayenne pepper

= hot red pepper flakes

= chili powder

PICKLING SPICE (⅔ cup)

4 cinnamon sticks (each about
   3 inches long)

1 piece of dried ginger root (about
   1 inch long)

2 Tablespoons mustard seed

2 teaspoons whole allspice

2 teaspoons black peppercorns

2 teaspoons whole cloves

2 teaspoons dill seed

2 teaspoons coriander seed

2 teaspoons whole mace, crumbled

8 bay leaves, crumbled

1 whole, dried red pepper,
   about 1½ inches long, chopped

PIE SPICE (apple or pumpkin)

½ teaspoon cinnamon

¼ teaspoon nutmeg

⅛ teaspoon allspice

⅛ teaspoon cardamom

PORT

= Madeira

= sherry

POULTRY SEASONING

> 2 Tablespoons dried marjoram
> 2 teaspoons dried parsley
> 2 Tablespoons dried savory
> 1 Tablespoon dried sage
> 1½ teaspoons dried thyme

ROSEMARY

> = marjoram
> = oregano

RUM

> = brandy
> = cognac

SAFFLOWER (or AZAFRAN)

> = saffron (use only a tiny bit)

SAFFRON (1 teaspoon)

> = 1 Tablespoon dried yellow marigold petals
> = azafran (also called safflower; use much more)

SAGE

> = rosemary
> = oregano

SASSAFRAS (also known as GUMBO FILÉ)

SUMMER SAVORY
= thyme (optional: add sage)

SALT
To flavor foods without salt, add to foods one (or more) of following:

black pepper

garlic

onion powder

mustard powder

paprika

red pepper

lemon juice

vinegar

wine (not cooking wines)

SEASONED SALT
1 cup salt

2½ teaspoons paprika

2 teaspoons dry mustard

1½ teaspoons oregano

1 teaspoon garlic powder

½ teaspoon onion powder

(continued)

OR:
    ½ cup salt
    1 teaspoon paprika
    1 teaspoon dry mustard
    1 teaspoon oregano
    1 teaspoon garlic powder
    ½ teaspoon onion powder

SESAME SEED
= finely-chopped almonds

SHERRY
= Madeira
= port

SPIRITS
See notes at beginning of chapter
See LIQUEURS

STAR ANISE (anise seed)
= fennel seed

SUMAC
= lemongrass
= lemon

TARRAGON
= chervil (use more)
= parsley (use more)

THYME

> = marjoram
>
> = oregano
>
> = bay leaf

TURMERIC

> = mustard powder (optional: plus saffron)

VERBENA

> = lemon peel
>
> = lemongrass

VINEGAR (up to 3 tablespoons)

> = lemon juice
>
> **NOTE:** for marinade, use wine and omit sugar and water

WHISKEY

> = bourbon

WINE (½ cup for marinade)

= ¼ cup vinegar, plus 1 Tablespoon sugar plus ¼ cup water

Also see notes at beginning of chapter

MEAT, FISH AND POULTRY

No, this isn't a list of what to substitute instead of meat; rather, it's about which meat to use when they're out of something at your local market, or what seafood to buy when you discover the one you wanted is out of season.

Specific fish are listed according to the way(s) they're commonly cooked: as fillets, as steaks, or as whole fish (after being cleaned, of course), under "FISH" in this chapter.

Incidentally, you may also be surprised at how much money you can save with the knowledge of what to substitute for expensive cuts like veal or swordfish.

BACON

= ham, in cooking

GROUND BEEF

= ground turkey

= ground pork

= ground veal

= ground lamb

NOTE: combinations of beef and these substitutes can also be used in most recipes

CHICKEN

= rabbit (in pieces)

= Cornish game hen

= turkey

CHICKEN BREASTS, BONELESS

= turkey breast slices

= veal scallops

COCKLES

= small clams

CORNISH GAME HEN

= squab

= quail

CRAYFISH

= small lobster

= prawns

= langouste (langoustine)

FISH FILLETS

The following are often cooked as fillets:

bluefish

catfish

cod

flounder

haddock

halibut

John Dory

mahi mahi

monkfish

orange roughy

pike

pollock

red snapper

sandab

scrod

trout

turbot

FISH STEAKS

The following are often cooked as steaks:

ahi

cod

halibut

John Dory

salmon

sea bass

shark

swordfish

tuna

WHOLE FISH

The following are often cooked whole:

bass

catfish

flounder

halibut

mackerel

pike

salmon

swordfish

tuna

turbot

PEPPERONI

> = sausage (cooked)
>
> = salami

GROUND PORK

> = sausage meat (and omit salt and other spices from recipe)

PORK FAT (fresh)

> = salt pork, boiled briefly; omit salt from recipe
>
> = unsmoked bacon, boiled briefly; omit salt from recipe

PRAWNS

> = shrimp

PROSCIUTTO

> = smoked ham

QUAIL

> = Cornish game hen
>
> = squab

RABBIT

> = chicken (pieces)

SALAMI

> = pepperoni

SARDINES (commonly processed)
= small herring

= small mackerel

SAUSAGE
= pepperoni

= ground pork with sage, marjoram, garlic and onions to taste.

SCALLOPS
= shark

SHRIMP
= prawns

SQUAB
= Cornish game hen

= chicken (halves)

= pigeon

= quail

TUNA (canned)
= albacore

= cooked, boned chicken

VEAL SCALLOPS
> = boned, skinned chicken breasts
> = turkey breast slices

VIENNA SAUSAGE
> = frankfurter

VEGETABLES

Vegetables are vegetables, and everyone knows which ones they like—right? Of course. Only now once-rare gourmet items appear in recipes coast-to-coast as our every day cooking becomes more adventuresome (and often confusing).

The enemies of vegetables are time, heat and light. If you feel your vegetables are not as fresh as they might be, add a dash of lemon juice to the cooking water. And for taste and nutrition, it's best to minimize the amount of water and cooking time you use.

ACORN SQUASH
   = butternut squash
   = pumpkin

ALFALFA SPROUTS
   = watercress

ARTICHOKE HEART
   = Jerusalem artichoke (also known as sunchoke)
   = kohlrabi (cooked)

ARUGULA
(also known as ROCKET)
   = Belgian endive
   = dandelion greens
   = endive
   = escarole

BEAN SPROUTS
   = celery

BEET GREENS
   See GREENS

BELGIAN ENDIVE
   = fennel

BORAGE

> = cucumber (especially in dishes with yogurt)

BROCCOLI DE RABE
> **See GREENS**

BUTTERNUT SQUASH

> = acorn squash
>
> = pumpkin

CABBAGE

> = Chinese cabbage
>
> = lettuce
>
> = kohlrabi

CARROT

> = parsnip

CAULIFLOWER

> = kohlrabi

CELERIAC (also known as CELERY ROOT)
> = kohlrabi

CELERY

> = green pepper
>
> = jicama
>
> = bean sprouts
>
> = Belgian endive
>
> = fennel

CELERY ROOT (also known as CELERIAC)

CHARD

> **See GREENS**

CHILI PEPPERS (also known as CHILE PEPPERS)

> **NOTE:** These vary greatly in strength from mild to extra-hot, so use care when attempting substitutions.

CHINESE CABBAGE

> = cabbage
>
> = lettuce

CHIVES

> **See GREEN ONIONS**

COLLARD GREENS

> **See GREENS**

DAIKON

> = radish

DANDELION GREENS
    See GREENS

ENDIVE (also known as CURLY ENDIVE)
    = chicory
    = escarole
    = Belgian endive

ESCAROLE
    = arugula
    = endive

FAVA BEANS
    = lima beans

FENNEL (Florentine)
    = Belgian endive
    = celery

GARLIC (1 clove)
    = ¼ teaspoon minced, dried garlic
    = ⅓ teaspoon garlic powder
    = ½ teaspoon minced garlic
      (from jar)
    **See HERBS, SPICES AND FLAVORINGS
    CHAPTER**

GREEN BEANS
    = wax beans

GREEN ONION

= scallion

= leek

= shallot (use less)

= chives

Also see HERBS, SPICES AND FLAVORINGS CHAPTER

GREEN PEPPER

= celery

= red pepper

= yellow pepper

GREENS (also known as LEAFY GREENS)

= beet greens (milder)

= collard greens (milder)

= broccoli de rabe (milder)

= rapini (also known as broccoli de rabe)

= chard (medium mild)

= kale (medium mild)

= spinach (medium mild)

= Swiss chard (also known as chard)

= dandelion greens (stronger)

= mustard greens (stronger)

= turnip greens (stronger)

JERUSALEM ARTICHOKE (also known as SUNCHOKE)
= artichoke heart

JICAMA
= raw turnip

= water chestnuts

KIDNEY BEANS
= pink beans

= pinto beans

= red beans

NOTE: these are smaller

KALE
See GREENS

KOHLRABI
= cauliflower

= artichoke heart

= cabbage

= celeriac

= radish

LEEKS
= shallots

= onions (use less)

LETTUCE
> = cabbage
> = Chinese cabbage

LIMA BEANS
> = fava beans

MUNG BEANS
> = split peas

MUSHROOMS (½ lb. fresh)
> = 6 ounces, canned, drained

MUSTARD GREENS
> See GREENS

OKRA
> = eggplant (though texture will be different)

ONION (1 small white or yellow)

= red onion (not usually for cooking)

= 1 Tablespoon instant minced onion

= 1 Tablespoon onion flakes

= ¼ cup frozen chopped onion

= 1 teaspoon onion powder

= shallots (use more)

= leeks (use a little more)

PARSLEY ROOT

= parsnip

PARSNIP

= parsley root

= carrot

PATTYPAN SQUASH (also known as SUMMER SQUASH)

= yellow crookneck squash

= yellow straightneck squash

= zucchini

PINK BEANS

= pinto beans

= red beans

= kidney beans (these are larger)

PINTO BEANS

> = pink beans
>
> = red beans
>
> = kidney beans (these are larger)

PUMPKIN

> = acorn squash
>
> = butternut squash

RAPINI

> **See GREENS**

RED BEANS

> = pinto beans
>
> = pink beans
>
> = kidney beans (these are larger)

RED CABBAGE

> = cabbage (green)

RED ONION

> = onion

RED PEPPER

> = green pepper
>
> = yellow pepper
>
> **NOTE:** this is for bell pepper, *not* chili pepper

ROCKET

> See ARUGULA

SCALLIONS

> = onions (use less)
> = shallots
> = leeks
> = green onions

SHALLOTS

> = onions (use less)
> = leeks
> = green onions
> = scallions

SORREL

> = spinach

SPINACH

> See GREENS

SPLIT PEAS

> = mung beans

SUMMER SQUASH (also known as PATTYPAN SQUASH)

= yellow crookneck squash

= yellow straightneck squash

= zucchini

SUNCHOKES (also known as JERUSALEM ARTICHOKES)

SUNFLOWER SPROUTS

= watercress

SWEET POTATO

= yam

TOMATOES (1 cup, canned)

= 1⅓ cup chopped fresh tomatoes, simmered

TOMATOES (1 lb., cooked, seasoned)

= 8 ounces tomato sauce, to use in cooking

TRUFFLES (fresh)

= canned truffles or canned truffle peels; add canning liquid

TURNIP (cooked)

= rutabaga

TURNIP (raw)
= jicama
= radish

TURNIP GREENS
See GREENS

WATER CHESTNUTS
= jicama (raw)

WATERCRESS
= sunflower sprouts

WAX BEANS
= green beans

WHITE BEANS
= pea beans
= navy beans

WHITE ONION
= yellow onion

YAM
= sweet potato

YELLOW CROOKNECK SQUASH
> = pattypan squash
> = yellow straightneck squash
> = zucchini

YELLOW PEPPER
> = green pepper
> = red pepper

YELLOW ONION
> = white onion

YELLOW STRAIGHTNECK SQUASH
> = pattypan squash
> = yellow crookneck squash
> = zucchini

ZUCCHINI
> = pattypan squash
> = yellow crookneck squash
> = yellow straightneck squash

TOO MUCH

Sometimes, instead of not having a particular ingredient at all, you have the opposite problem: you end up with too much of something. The following is designed to remedy common kitchen disasters of this type.

ALCOHOL

If too much in punch or other mixed alcoholic drinks, float thin slice of cucumber to absorb taste of alcohol

FAT (in stew or soup or gravy)

Drop in ice cubes and grease will stick to them; remove quickly.

OR wrap ice cubes in paper towels and draw over the surface; fat will begin to solidify and stick to the paper towel; repeat until enough fat is removed.

OR place paper towel lightly on surface; let it absorb fat; remove; repeat as necessary.

OR use a flat lettuce leaf the same way.

OR refrigerate dish, then skim solidified fat from top; then continue with recipe.

GARLIC

Simmer a sprig or a small bunch of parsley in stew or soup for ten minutes

KETCHUP, in a sauce

Add lemon juice to mask some of
the ketchupy taste.

NOTE: you may add a bit of sugar to
cut acidity.

SALT

Peel a potato; slice thin; add to dish
and boil until transparent; remove
potato.

OR if fish is too salty, add vinegar to
cooking liquid.

OR, if tomato dish, add more peeled
tomatoes to absorb salt; leave in
dish if appropriate.

OR for processed items like soup, stew
or tomato sauce, add pinches of
brown sugar to taste.

TOMATO

See KETCHUP

WATER, especially for sauces, soups and stews

Boil gently until food has reached
proper consistency.

HOUSEHOLD FORMULAS

Remember how your grandmother used to give you helpful cleaning hints—only now you can't recall any of them?

And you know what it feels like to be standing in the supermarket, not wanting to spend a small fortune on the latest specialty cleanser just to see if maybe it works.

Well, look down this list, and chances are you'll find a tried-and-true recipe for just what you need.

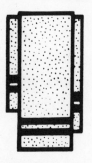

BATHROOM CLEANSER

Dip damp sponge in baking soda.

BRASS CLEANSER

Rub hard with lemon juice and salt.
Or spread with ketchup. Let stand
10 minutes and rub hard.

BREADBOX CLEANSER

2 Tablespoons vinegar in 1 quart
water. (Deters mold, too.)

COPPER CLEANSER

Make a paste of lemon juice, salt
and flour. Or spread with ketchup.
Let stand 10 minutes and rub
hard.

CRYSTAL CLEANSER

Half rubbing alcohol, half water; do
not rinse.

DRAIN FRESHENER

1 cup baking soda poured down
the drain; after 2 minutes pour in
1 cup vinegar, then 2 quarts
boiling water.

ELECTRIC IRON STAIN REMOVER

Equal parts vinegar and salt.

FLOOR WAX
½ cup cornstarch in 1 gallon luke-warm water.

FURNITURE POLISH
⅓ cup boiled linseed oil
⅓ cup turpentine
⅓ cup vinegar

HARD WATER DEPOSIT REMOVER
Soak item in white vinegar or a half-and-half solution of white vinegar and water.

NON-STICK PAN CLEANSER
Baking soda on non-abrasive scouring pad.

OVEN CLEANSER
(for non-self-cleaning ovens)
Pour ½ cup ammonia into a bowl. Set in cold oven over night. Next morning, mix the ammonia with 1 quart warm water and clean off inside of oven.

POT AND PAN CLEANSER
Soak in white vinegar 30 minutes.

REFRIGERATOR CLEANSER

1 Tablespoon powdered borax in
   1 quart water

OR 1 teaspoon baking soda in
   1 quart water.

SILVER CLEANSER

Make paste of baking soda and
   water. Apply with damp sponge or
   cloth and continue rubbing until
   clean.

STAINLESS STEEL CLEANSER

Ammonia and hot water, mixed with
   mild, non-chlorinated cleanser.

OR, to remove spots, rub with cloth
   dampened with white vinegar.

WINDOW CLEANSER

½ cup white or cider vinegar in
   ½ gallon water; spray on and
   wipe with crumpled newspaper.

OR 1 Tablespoon ammonia in
   water (and use gloves while you
   clean).

WOODWORK CLEANSER

1 teaspoon white vinegar in 1 quart water.

WOODWORK (VARNISHED), FURNITURE or GLASS CLEANSER

Tea, steeped 30 to 40 minutes.

INDEX

INDEX

Also of interest from the Globe Pequot Press: